A
Clearer
Vision

Lenten
Midweek Sermons

David Belgum

CSS Publishing Company, Inc., Lima, Ohio

Copyright © 2000 by
CSS Publishing Company, Inc.
Lima, Ohio

Unless marked otherwise scripture quotations are from the *New Revised Standard Version of the Bible*, copyright 1989 by the Division of Christian Education of the National Council of the Churches of Christ in the USA. Used by permission.

Scripture quotations marked (RSV) are from the *Revised Standard Version of the Bible*, copyrighted 1946, 1952 ©, 1971, 1973, by the Division of Christian Education of the National Council of the Churches of Christ in the USA. Used by permission.

This book is available in the following formats, listed by ISBN:
0-7880-1537-0   Book
0-7880-1538-9   Disk
0-7880-1539-7   Sermon Prep

PRINTED IN U.S.A.

Dedicated to
Bethany Lutheran Church
West Branch, Iowa

Table Of Contents

Introduction

While I was lecturing in Ireland recently, I was introduced to an ancient method of Reading the Word in preparation for hearing the sermon the following week. My host, who shared it, is Father Brendan Clifford, a Dominican, who was my student 25 years ago. It is called *Lectio Divina* and goes as follows in three steps.

1. *Read* the text aloud and *hear* the words. Divide the text into smaller sections. Who were the people involved and what were they doing? Maybe they were shepherds, fishermen, soldiers, priests, foreigners, men, women, outcasts, or persons of high station. How and why do you do some of these same things or make similar statements? What does it mean to be criticized, to persecute or to put down someone else as was done in the text? Insert yourself thus into the text two or three times during the week, reading the text afresh.

2. *Meditate* on the passage during the week while you are doing routine work — washing dishes or waiting for the grain drier to stop, while driving to work or waiting in line, while riding the school bus, and so forth. In other words, mix it into your daily life here and now. Let your feelings, imagination, creative fantasy, and putting yourself into the text mix with the factual reading of the account. Then the story does not just belong to Saint Luke or Saint Matthew or Saint Paul; you appropriate it and incorporate it into your own self, and it becomes your story as well. Not only (a) this did happen; but also (b) how is it happening today? and, remember (c) *this always happens.*

3. *Pray* guided by the text. Several kinds of prayer might grow out of this experience: Thanksgiving, Humility, Petition, Repentance, Acceptance, Praise, and so on.

So often we read or study the Bible as a textbook, looking for information for the conscious mind. In this approach we also let our feelings, memories, associations, dreams, and emotions float up to the surface as well as thinking about the cognitive meaning of a particular text. This allows your Reading the Word to permeate your whole person and helps to make the text your own. Please do this with each reading in the booklet before reading the sermon for that day.

Matthew 6:1-6, 16-18
Ash Wednesday

Wanting To Be Seen

Theatron is the word we translate as "to be seen." In the theater, on the stage, that is the whole purpose, to be seen. On the stage is where persons legitimately pretend (*hypocrisis*) to be someone other than what they are in real life. It is perfectly okay for Billy Smith to pretend to be Robin Hood in the school play. It is even announced in the program that Billy will "play the part" of Robin Hood. The play would be a big success if the audience were so lost in the action that they actually thought of the lad as Robin Hood and forgot all about his really being Billy Smith.

Offstage, in real life, Jesus cautions against pretending to be something other than who or what we really are. Don't pretend to be generous in almsgiving when you are doing it only for show. "Hey, look at me (ta-ta-ta-tat-ta-da sounded on your trumpet), I'm about to give a few pennies to this poor beggar. How about that?" Jesus so often saw behind the deed to the motive, the real intention of a person. The same goes for prayer and religiosity in general:

> And whenever you pray, do not be like the hypocrites;
> for they love to stand and pray in the synagogues and
> at the street corners, so that they may be seen by others. Truly, I tell you, they have received their reward.
> — Matthew 6:5

Even in prayer they want to be on center stage (*theatron*). Then Jesus proceeded to teach them a simple Jewish prayer. We call it the Lord's Prayer.

Have you ever wondered if Jesus were contradicting himself? Earlier in this Sermon on the Mount he said this:

> You are the light of the world. A city built on a hill cannot be hid. No one after lighting a lamp puts it under a bushel basket, but on the lampstand, and it gives light

9

to all in the house. In the same way, let your light shine
before others, so that they may see your good works,
and give glory to your Father in heaven.
                                        — Matthew 5:14-16

There is something to be said for being a good role model. No need to hide from your children the fact that you pay your taxes honestly and treat customers helpfully in your shop or office. Amidst all the negative and destructive news, we hear a cheery little story. A boy, age fourteen, sent a thousand dollars to President Clinton to help with the deficit. That "good work" may well have caused a great many wealthy people to withhold their complaints about helping out with higher taxes for the same end. We need positive role models of any age to raise our sights.

Maybe those two statements of Jesus need not be contradictory. Remember we need to bear in mind the motive. Jesus said if others see your genuine good works they may be led to glorify God, who, after all, blessed you with such an opportunity.

Case #1 George Washington

Richard Norton Smith recently published a thorough and sensitive biography titled *Patriarch: George Washington and the New American Nation*. Chapter 5 has a title that is relevant to this sermon: "To See and Be Seen." The opening paragraph clearly explains Washington's motivation for being seen so much in public.

> *Politics is theater, and George Washington was America's first actor-president. The Constitution made Washington head of state as well as head of the government, and no man had a better grasp of ceremonial leadership than George III's American usurper. The Washington presidency was nothing if not theatrical. Why else the elaborate rituals of levee and drawing room, in triumphal progress to occasions of state and deferential response from lawmakers for whom the president was both symbol of continuity and instrument of change? As the embodiment of revolutionary virtue, Washington knew that whenever he appeared, partisan*

murmurs would be lost in a chorus of hero worship.
This alone was enough to make him the young republic's
greatest asset and only glue.

In March of 1791 Washington took off on a 1,700-mile tour of southern states to apply some of that "glue" to hold together separate states which had more interest in their own affairs than the country as a whole. It was a crucial time when "states' rights" could have predominated over the welfare of the union of the thirteen colonies. Although Washington enjoyed the out-of-doors and the adventure of this journey, he saw it as an obligation to contribute his reputation and the public adoration ascribed to him as part of his civic obligation. Personally, he would rather have taken a week off here and there to attend to his beloved plantation at Mount Vernon. There he was, for over four months, staying in a different town practically every evening, being introduced to fifty or sixty ladies at a fancy ball and listening to endless welcoming speeches that sooner or later all began sounding alike. It wasn't what you would call fun.

Now George had grown up in the Episcopal Church and had no doubt heard this very text preached about a few times as well as other admonitions to humility and avoiding the sin of pride. He was not using this tour for his personal gain. He saw his very personality, his past successes as emancipator, and his charismatic influence as tools or resources for holding a fragile country together. He preferred not to be president, and wanted to return to his large farm after his tour of military duty was over. He also resisted any effort to make him a kind of king.

We come again to the question of motive. He deliberately allowed himself to "be seen" maybe more than anyone else in the colonies; but it was not hypocrisy. He sensed that what was called for was to allow himself to be used as a symbol, much like a flag is carried conspicuously in a parade. To have drifted back into the comfortable shadows of privacy would not have been humility as much as a denial of his vocation. We need to look not only at behavior on the surface but also to ask what it means and what its purpose is.

11

Case #2 My Humble Self

Common folk wisdom is that a Norwegian is a person who goes about asking, "Excuse me, am I occupying space you should have? Am I breathing too much of your oxygen?" If I was told once it was a hundred times, "Don't put yourself forward; don't be pushy." As Director of the Department of Pastoral Services at University Hospital, I quickly realized that I needed to be a salesman. Whenever I spoke before a group, it was also mentioned that I was from the Department of Pastoral Services at University Hospital. If I did a good job and made, excuse me, a good "impression," that helped the reputation and visibility of the Department of Pastoral Services.

Our staff was made up of clergy who had changed roles quite drastically. Whereas formerly, as parish pastors, they had been conspicuous in the community, up front by the altar and in the raised pulpit, wearing colorful stoles, and so on, now they were at one sick bed at a time as their parish. It surely was not the same kind of ego support they had received as such a special person in the congregation and community. The notoriety was missing. One denomination even listed hospital chaplains as "nonproductive" or some such category, years ago, since they were not generating income for the budget. It is not easy going from "being seen" to "not being seen."

I once told my colleagues that sometimes when I felt unnoticed or bypassed, I would send in an article to the paper or in some other way "let my light shine." The following week someone in the hospital or community would comment that they had seen my article or heard my course over the radio. My hope, every now and then realized, was that this would help to publicize the work of the Department of Pastoral Services. Sometimes it even generated financial support for the programs.

I sometimes submit articles, essays, or letters to our local *West Branch Times*. At the end it says, "submitted by David Belgum, Pastor of Bethany Lutheran Church." Again, some subtle, free advertising for the church. I want the name of our church to "be seen" as often as is decent and within the bounds of good ecumenical relations.

12

You may well ask, "How do you know your motive is pure, since Jesus is so concerned about motive and intention?" Frankly, I doubt if our motives, either George's or mine, are ever 100 percent pure. Even when we do a genuine kindness, we usually get a lot back in return. Maybe it is impossible to answer. If my motives were anywhere between 75 percent and 85 percent pure, I'd be quite satisfied. God knows me better than I know myself. Fortunately, he exercises a lot of grace and understanding, forgiveness, and whatever else I need to make up the difference, so I don't really have to worry about it.

Case #3 You

Now it is your turn to focus on what it means to *you* to "be seen" or to "let your light shine." Is it useful in your case; does it feel right? How do you know where you fall on a scale of arrogantly showing off on the one extreme or hiding your light under a bushel basket on the other hand? What could you do to motivate yourself in a more wholesome direction if that is what your self-analysis calls for? What if you discover that you are not perfectly genuine in your motivation?

Here we are at the beginning of Lent, a time traditionally set aside for self-examination and reflection, a time to sit back and relax quietly, to look at our lives in an unhurried way, without defensiveness or the need to prove anything at all. It should be a nonthreatening time because God is not out to get us. Rather our Creator wants to support us on our journey through life. Jesus teaches us again and again the things that can enrich our lives. When he points out pitfalls and temptations, it is done lovingly because he desires our welfare.

Some consider Lent a time to give up something they like. It would be no great sacrifice to give up hypocrisy. It doesn't really do us much good anyway. And showing off and bragging about our virtues and good deeds doesn't really win friends and influence people. Lent can also be a time to thank God for golden opportunities to pass on the blessings we have so freely received as we actively search out ways of being a service to others, to be a blessing, to let our light shine, so that others may see our good works, and give glory to our Father in heaven. May we have a clearer vision as we set out on our Lenten journey. Amen.

Genesis 2:7-9, 3:1-7; Matthew 4:1-11
Lent — Week 1

Adam And Jesus See Temptation

Adam and Jesus were both good and created in the Image of God. It was not inherent evil or original sin that blinded Adam. We read that "God saw everything that he had made, and behold it was very good"; that included fish, birds, cattle, creeping things, and Adam. "Thus the heavens and the earth were finished, and all the host of them." Nothing was lacking. Everything was going along just fine.

How like us. All our needs are met and supplied. Chances are very good we have a weather-tight house with a thermostat to turn on the furnace or air conditioning, a refrigerator to keep our food in a good state of preservation, a bed with a mattress on top of a spring and enough bed covers to keep us comfortable within a fully insulated bedroom. Total® cereal provides us with 100 percent of our vitamin requirements and enough fiber in each serving to last us a week. If we need to get up in the middle of the night for some reason, we have only to go down the hall a few steps to meet our needs and right handy is tissue paper as soft as a white cloud. Yes, we have it good here in America.

Adam's situation was much like ours. He was surrounded by a rich diet of fish, meat, fruit, grains; all available just for the very slight work of picking them as needed. His clothing budget was nil since the climate was so mild in the Garden of Eden. He had no mortgage, nothing to worry about. He could cavort around the Garden in the daytime and sleep soundly at night because he had no need for sleeping pills to soothe his mind uncluttered by worry about stress, job security, loss of health and pension benefits, tenure, seniority, promotions, or status. Oh, it was a good life. One would think he would have been happy as a clam. I would have been; wouldn't you?

Unfortunately, Adam did have one problem, which wasn't really his fault. He happened to come along in that critical stage of evolutionary development God was using to process his creation into ever more complex levels of existence. All those critters below him in the developmental chain were governed by instinct and really were not confronted with many genuine choices. Cows and elephants ate when they got hungry and stopped eating when the instinct of hunger was satisfied. The bull did basically the same without gluttony of either of his two basic appetites. It did not even occur to him, in what we today would call a temptation, to kill young calves and then have sex with them. The cycle of seasons, both of biology and nature, worked so smoothly that even our most wild-eyed ecologists would have been well pleased with how things were going.

There was no danger of Adam's breaking any commandments because none of them applied to him whatsoever. Theft was not an issue because God had already given him dominion over everything to plant, pen up, eat — do with as he wished as long as he was a responsible steward. Things were so elemental that it was almost impossible to foul up. To whom or about whom would he have borne false witness anyway? He had no neighbors of his own kind nor any houses or cars to covet. Profanity was almost totally unnecessary. There were better ways to call the cattle or otherwise order things about. He didn't really need a sabbath for rest since God had provided him with a period of darkness every 24 hours; and since there was no cable television nor places open late at night, there was not much to do except just call it a day and have a good night's sleep. The reason Adam slept so well was that there was also nothing bothering his conscience. Oh, I'm getting ahead of the story.

We need to back up to the matter of God's creative program of complexification. Adam was developing faster in one part of his body than any other animal. He was getting a big head. His brain began to whirl and spin with remarkable speed as little neurons, protons, atoms, and molecules interacted with each other and formed strings and connections back and forth within his skull. Like a little telephone company, communications began interacting and sending out messages that gave Adam his first really severe Excedrin® headache. One by one the Seven Deadly Sins began to loom up as possibilities before his eyes. His vision became clouded and he began to be unable to focus on his original job description: "have dominion over the fish of the sea, and over the birds of the air, and over the cattle, and over all the earth, and every creeping thing that creeps upon the earth." He was not content with his job of farming and wildlife management; he wanted to get into government, which he felt had more status.

Enter: The Big Temptation. There was a promise that he could become a co-equal with God, more than vice president, actually God's equal in wisdom and power, creativity, you name it. It was not even a close relative like a monkey or gorilla who tempted him, but a sneaky snake in the grass, the lowest form of life. Actually the writer of Genesis tries to go easy on Adam, saying that a conniving person passed the message to Adam secondhand. Yes, so often temptation comes as supposedly someone else's idea. "How about a drink? You don't have a problem with alcohol, do you?" someone asks. As often as not, the person replies, "That's what my spouse says and nags me a lot." The more gossips the temptation passes through the less clear the responsibility seems. Finally, "Don't blame me; it wasn't my idea in the first place."

There were other ways in which Adam's head and brain were getting him into trouble. He could see new connections and possibilities. Not only did bananas satisfy his hunger; they tasted good. He got into eating them long after his hunger was satisfied. Bang! He was hooked on another of the Seven Deadly Sins — Gluttony. He went downhill so fast after that it was pitiful. He not only lost the farm, but was kicked way into the next county and told never to come back to Paradise again.

Yes, friends, we have been stuck with the Old Adam ever since, repeating his mistakes, his arrogant grab for power and status. Look around you; it's not a pretty picture. Adam desperately needed a clearer vision of who he was and what his place in the universe should be. It is still true of us today. Our job is not to be God or even pretend we are. It's no good complaining and saying, "Oh shucks, I'm just a person, a little creature in this vast universe." Rather let us hear the good news that God has created us in his image and has a wonderful job description for us. We can hear that call to vocation if we are not distracted by some snake in the grass.

Jesus was also confronted by temptation. He differed a great deal from Adam. For one thing, he had a clearer vision, a clear vision of who he was and what his vocation was. Maybe that is why he could see temptation coming. The Tempter was not able to catch him by surprise. And out in the desert there was no one else to blame. He was alone with the Tempter. Sometimes we also realize that we are alone with no one else to blame. We are most vulnerable when in solitude. Yet, Jesus was not totally alone. He was with God and God was with him. In the very verse before this story of the forty days in the wilderness, we read this testimony and validation of his identity. Immediately after Jesus' baptism, he heard these words, "This is my beloved Son, with whom I am well pleased."

Actually the original word, often translated as temptation, is *peirazein.* It means "to test." In our materials engineering laboratory at the university, we test and stress beams to the breaking point. That way we will know how much a bridge, or library floor holding up tons of books, can actually support. But even on the cross, Jesus was not broken down.

1. **Instant gratification** is as familiar to us as today's mail. We want immediate solutions without even working for them. "Are you hungry, Jesus? Snap your fingers and these oblong loaf-shaped stones will turn into bread." Jesus replied something to the effect that it is as important how you get the bread as is the bread itself. Life is more than bread. Some of our drug dealers do not understand this when they demand, "Give me the bread, man!" And a meaningless life can devour bread, steak, champagne, and prostitutes. Oh, you can get a lot of stuff with money. You can satisfy every instinct in your body and still not be as well off as the critters of Adam's day who had no further obligations than to obey animal instinct. But we can't turn the clock back. Today we are responsible to know the difference between bread and the Bread of Life. Jesus said he wanted us to have life and have it abundantly, not just the humble food that the snake in the grass lived on in his very small world. Jesus also said that if we drank of the water he could

offer us we would never thirst again. "One does not live by bread alone, but by every word that comes from the mouth of God" (Matthew 4:4b).

2. **Be spectacular** is the second test of Jesus' character. The Tempter suggested that Jesus demonstrate his divine capacity and ability by doing the aerial act of all times. Even nineteen hundred years later, Barnum and Bailey Circus did not advertise a high wire act without a net and also without a wire. Jesus was urged to leap from the top of the Temple in Jerusalem. It was ninety cubits from the pinnacle to the courtyard (a little taller than the average town water tower). But if one were to jump off the other side into the Valley of Kidron (between the Temple Mount and the Mount of Olives), it could be a fall of 450 feet. Take your choice.

What if Jesus had made that spectacular jump and landed safely as the Tempter quoted? "He will give his angels charge of you, and on their hands they will bear you up, lest you strike your foot against a stone" (Matthew 4:6b-c *RSV*). Jesus would have been known as Number One in track and field and would surely have represented Judea at the Olympics in Greece. Bumper stickers would abound: "Jump Like Jesus," "No One Can Jump Like Jesus," "Jump For Joy." He would have been famous throughout the Roman Empire for jumping. Young Saul might have gone to the great games in Tarsus to see Jesus jump across the entire stadium during halftime. No kidding, remember what a sensation Evel Knievel made when he proposed to jump across a canyon on his motorcycle? You can get a lot of mileage out of being far out and spectacular. Jesus chose not to make that his mission in life. Superman is better suited to a comic book than real life. He said that would be turning the tables and tempting God, testing God to see how much he would put up with before yanking Jesus' credentials. "You shall not tempt the Lord your God."

Aren't we tempted and tested in the same way occasionally? We might enjoy notoriety for its own sake even when it is not related in any way to a useful project or service of others. Most of us lead rather ordinary lives and have modest abilities and capabilities, so maybe it is a rather rare temptation. You be the judge for yourself. If you should be "lucky" enough to become famous, that is time enough to worry about this problem; but also by that time you may already have become a bit intoxicated with the fame and rather full of yourself. That makes it even harder to ace the test objectively and make the moral hurdle.

3. **The end justifies the means** has often been a rationalization when compromise seems the only way out. Just imagine how much good Jesus would have been able to accomplish if he had accepted the Tempter's offer of all the kingdoms of the world. He would have been Emperor of Rome and with one word could have stopped the carnage of gladiators and other sports like having wild animals eat people in the Circus at Rome for the entertainment of the bored citizens. If he were political ruler of all those countries of the known world there wouldn't have to be any more Babylonian Captivity, Egyptian slave exploitation, wars of territorial expansionism; oh, he could have done so much good in such a position of influence and power. What could be better than a benevolent despot? But he had another agenda in mind — the Kingdom of God. Instead, we read, he walked along the Sea of Galilee preaching, "Repent, for the kingdom of heaven is at hand."

How can you and I judge when some compromise is legitimate? Maybe you are 100 percent for a piece of legislation, but it cannot pass because two factions have certain objections and propose amendments. Well, let's be realistic; maybe some of their ideas are useful. We need to be humble about our proposals and open-minded. Where do we draw the line and why? The key is in our text: "if you will fall down and worship me." Martyrs of all ages have willingly laid down their lives rather than turn their backs on their God and God's clearly expressed will for their lives. "Begone, Satan! for it is written, 'You shall worship the Lord your God, and him only shall you serve' " (Matthew 4:10 *RSV*).

The test in this third instance is one of ultimate loyalty. Whom do you worship? What has the highest priority in your life? Once it was clear where Jesus stood concerning worship, the Tempter just gave up and left him alone. There is no point in pursuing the testing any further. Once a person is clear on worship of God, it is almost predictable what that person will say or how he or she will react to a number of other specific questions.

So what view should we take about temptation and testing? All school children know that without testing they will not be admitted or promoted to the next grade. If we are not tested, chances are we are not very alive, not very alert, not involved in the world and society around us. Facing the test head on and with God's support and grace, we become stronger for the exercise.

Second Sight

What was the experience high up on Mount Hermon, which we have come to call the Transfiguration of Jesus? When we modern, technologically-oriented westerners read, we expect to receive objective information that will benefit us and answer questions. We become uncomfortable when what we read raises questions or throws us for a loop.

All the symbolism of inspiration is packed into this short story. A bright light represented God's holiness and his blessing on those whom he had called. It is said of Jesus that "his face shone like the sun, and his clothes became dazzling white." It calls to mind how Moses' appearance changed when he came down from his encounter with God on Mount Sinai with the Ten Commandments in hand. "Moses did not know that his face shone because he had been talking with God. When Aaron and all the Israelites saw Moses, the skin of his face was shining and they were afraid to come hear him." That will happen when you are on a mountaintop with God. And, of course, we all remember the great prophet Elijah was caught up into the heights amidst the flashing light of a chariot of fire drawn by fiery horses. Martin Luther King, Jr., testified in his great speech, "I have been to the mountain."

We have also heard before about the bright cloud concealing and yet revealing God to the people of Israel. Sometimes it is "the cloud of unknowing" because the knowledge of God is hid from eyes not ready or willing to see. It resembles the "uncertainty principle." Yet people of faith among the Israelites did follow the pillar of fire by night and the pillar of cloud by day, and that brought them finally through their wilderness.

There is also in this story the familiar "coming down from the mountain." Transfiguration, or as the Greek word in the Bible, "metamorphosis," means change, not as an end in itself, but as a means to propel one forward into a new, a better life. In the case of

23

Moses this meant getting down to business and obeying the new Commandments of God for a better and more orderly life. In the case of Elijah it meant tossing the mantle down to Elisha so that the work could continue. To this day we speak of accepting the mantle of authority or this or that as an obligation, a calling. Jesus refused the luxury of staying in this mountaintop experience in the three booths the disciples offered to construct, a kind of Scout camp away from the city, the pleasures of being out in nature away from the hassles of the masses. "As they were coming down the mountain, Jesus commanded them, 'Tell no one the vision....' "

What Then Is A Vision?

Some would say that if something is a vision that means it just plain is not true. It did not really happen. It was an illusion (something that deceives by producing a false impression).

The fact of the matter is that there are many kinds of vision. The most elemental vision is physical. "I see a round, red ball six inches in diameter, period." Nothing more and nothing less. As the famous Detective Friday said, "Just give me the facts, ma'am!" This pertains to physical qualities that can be weighed, measured, counted, useful in science for comparing and classifying. Thus objects may be round, square, triangular, and so on.

Another sight deals with a different dimension of experience and meaning. I enjoy seeing my granddaughter swing her arms at random and finally strike the ball so that it goes rolling under the piano bench. We all clap our hands and say what a fine and bright girl she is. It is of little consequence whether the ball is red or blue, large or small. The game of it is the thing we are focusing on. Years later the same girl will be kicking a soccer ball in a high school match; and now it is all much more serious. This is the state championship tournament, and all hinges on her last kick in the final seconds of the game. Will it go through the goal? Hurray! She is not only a fine and bright girl now. She is going to get a big scholarship at her favorite university. Oh, yes, a ball can be seen in many ways.

There is another kind of vision or viewing things that "sees" into the future. *Successful Farming* tells the following story in its

March 1993, issue. Mr. Reeves began farming on a homestead near Garden City, Kansas, in the early 1900s. He *saw* the potential for a feedlot, which might well have been venturesome compared to neighbors with smaller herds. The story quickly moves on to his grandson, Lee Reeves, who is a visionary of our day. He has *seen* the potential for recycling that I found exciting. It goes something like this. He now feeds 17,000 cattle at a time. Meanwhile the run-off from the feedlot goes into a lagoon and is pumped back into the fields as fertilizer together with water irrigation. He converts a million bushels of milo a year into two-and-one-half million gallons of ethanol. The production of ethanol results in a large quantity of warm water in which fish thrive; so now he has produced 120,000 pounds of fresh fish for sale. The waste water from the fish is added to the irrigation water and goes back on the fields of corn and other crops; and the recycling starts all over. "Reeves *sees* a bright future for aquaculture." Ironically, the fish being produced are White Tilapia, the same fish Jesus fed the masses in biblical times. Reeves could not have done this without a vision. This vision includes imagination, creativity, and seeing potential in the future.

Second Sight In The Spiritual Sense

"Where there is no vision, the people perish ..." wrote the author of Proverbs. Another translation interprets it this way: "Where there is no prophecy the people cast off restraint." Here a vision refers to long-range sight and planning, aiming toward a goal. When a nation, or an individual for that matter, heads into the future toward a goal, some restraint is necessary, some self-discipline. The root of the word expressed by perish or casting off restraint means basically "letting go." An analogy would be that of driving horses pulling a carriage. If you let go of the reins the team may run every which way without guidance. They run across the ditch, over rocks at will. You will not reach your destination, if you ever had one. All restraint is cast off.

A people, and individuals who make up that people, need a vision or they wander about aimlessly, often repeating disastrous mistakes from their past history, going in circles. Prophetic persons can see further into the future than most of us; they can point the way. Throughout our Midwest, there were pioneers who had a vision that their district needed an academy, which later grew into a full-fledged college or university. At a Founders' Day banquet reference will be made to the vision of these early leaders in education. They saw a need and had vision of how the need was to be met. Sometimes it was lonely to be the only one in the community with this vision, this sense of fruitful destiny lying in the future, waiting to be realized. Daniel experienced this and reported it in his prophecy:

> ... I looked up and saw a man clothed in linen, with a belt of gold from Uphaz around his waist. His body was like beryl, his face like lightning, his eyes like flaming torches, his arms and legs like the gleam of burnished bronze, and the sound of his words like the roar of a multitude. I, Daniel, alone saw the vision; the people who were with me did not see the vision, though a great trembling fell upon them, and they fled and hid themselves.   — Daniel 10:6-7

And the messenger in the vision explained that he had come "to help you understand what is to happen to your people at the end of days."

Sometimes, when one has run out of reasons, logical explanations, careful planning, and all the rest, there suddenly dawns upon a person a new insight, a second sight. It may come in an unguarded moment, in a dream, in a vision, or when one is occupied with something totally unrelated. It is an "ah hah!" experience, an inspirational flash that seems to come out of thin air. The Bible is full of these reported experiences. Often this is called a "vision." As in Daniel's case, it is a bit lonely since no one else shares it. It therefore takes a lot of faith to trust it and its message. But we should be open to such inspirational intrusions into our regular life. It may even have been fermenting in our unconscious for some time and then breaks forth at the right time, or as Scripture says, "in the fullness of time."

Do not be discouraged if such a second sight does not come to you. Remember, Daniel was a rare case of prophecy. Jesus took only three out of the twelve to be with him on the mountain. That's only 25 percent. But we should receive it gladly and obediently if it should be our fate to be thus transformed or to see some helpful vision.

On the other hand, we should not be surprised if a vision should suddenly confront us. Some brilliant scientists have made their great breakthrough discoveries quite by accident. While pursuing one question, suddenly an answer to a much different question emerges as if from nowhere. We should also remember that Peter, James, and John were ordinary fishermen by background and trade. They were not noblemen, great generals, high up in government nor in academic circles.

We might be tempted to think that, because we are so ordinary, a life-transforming experience wouldn't possibly happen to us. We could block out the vision with our own arrogance, prejudice, or preconceived ideas, so that no new light could shine in upon our soul. You recall this was not the only vision Peter saw. He saw the sheet of food let down from on high, but unfortunately it was full of what the Hebrew tradition considered "unclean things." The Voice in his vision said, "What God made clean, you must not call profane." He immediately saw the light, had a second sight, saw the Gentiles in a new light because of his life-changing vision. From then on he saw that he must minister to the Gentiles as well as the Jews. It opened up a whole new pathway for the gospel to be spread. Maybe it never would have happened without such a vision. Peter was transformed. He gained much, but also lost something — his old smug sense of superiority; that was gone forever.

This happens among us today. You may have seen the transformation in the life of someone in your family or at your work or school. Whatever it was, something transformed that person from a pessimist to an optimist, from a self-centered person to an outgoing person, from being selfish and greedy to being generous and caring, from laziness to eager ambition. It may even have struck closer to home, in yourself, and you could mark the time and place of your transfiguration. You have shared the experience with others in all humility, passing it on as a blessing.

What is more, transfiguration, metamorphosis, always happens and will continue to happen whenever and wherever people of faith and expectation allow themselves to be exposed to a vision. I'm not saying we can make it happen by our will and effort. Rather we simply rejoice when Jesus invites us to a mountain and blesses us with a surprising vision — and then shows us where to go from there. Amen.

John 4:5-42
Lent — Week 3

Seeing The Whole Person

Not surprisingly, Jesus was dusty and thirsty under the noonday sun after his walk through the high hills and low mountains about forty miles north of Jerusalem. He had come as far as Sychar in the district of Samaria on his way to Galilee. The well near which he sat to rest has great symbolic significance for the story John is about to relate. It was Jacob's well, which means it went back to ancient Israel. Yes, the Samaritan woman even refers to it thus: "... our father Jacob, who gave us the well and drank from it himself." She also had enough Hebrew religious education to testify, "I know that Messiah is coming (he who is called Christ)." Near where she lived there had been a Samaritan temple; and she even gets into a discussion of which is the better place to worship, "on this mountain" or in Jerusalem.

How come, since the Judeans and the Samaritans seemed to have so much in common, had they reached such an impasse of bad relations? By the time of Jesus, not only should a Jewish man certainly not speak to a Samaritan woman, but very likely not to any other Samaritan as well. Jesus was definitely out of line here. Being a teacher of religion he should have known that these hill country folks were unclean pagans. Not only did it happen then, but it always happens. My group is better than your group. Back a century ago when this church was organized, there were two kinds of Lutheran immigrants from Denmark. You would think their common background and faith would have been a consolation so far from home; but no, the Holy Danes and the Happy Danes each considered themselves the better group and could not possibly cooperate. They formed separate synods, separate colleges, and separate seminaries, and each group sang out of its own hymnal. And this will always happen. Why? Because my group is better than your group, naturally. And I wouldn't be surprised but what you would say the same. We need a clearer vision.

29

How Did The Disciples See The Samaritan Woman?

Let us not be too hard on the disciples for adopting the standard prejudices of the day. I suppose they were like most redneck fishermen using stereotypes as a short cut way of judging character and worth. Can't you hear them bantering back and forth about passersby as they untangled their nets at the end of the day? "Oh, there goes another one; you know how they are." "I know the type; you can't count on 'em." "A Samaritan asked me if he could work on our fishing crew here on the Sea of Galilee. I said, 'No way, man!' I didn't want to start a fight; but I sure didn't want him hanging around." Did you catch me saying "redneck"? Isn't that stereotyping?

We must remember that, according to John's account, the disciples had only been in training a short while. There was the dramatic lesson at the wedding at Cana, when they really started believing in Jesus. Then there was the time they went on retreat at Capernaum for a few days. The encounter of Jesus with the money changers in the temple threw them for a loss. And maybe Jesus' counseling session with Nicodemus was confidential, and they hadn't been involved in that lesson. So here they were returning from downtown with the groceries for lunch when they stopped dead in their tracks. John reports that "they marveled that he was talking with a woman." No one asked, "Why are you talking with her?" or "Do you want to get us all in trouble? Have you forgotten? These are Samaritans up here — these hillbillies."

Impetuous Peter was quick to add his caution, as he would later when Jesus had to rebuke him, "Get behind me, Satan." Peter said, "Remember when the Judean Ku Klux Klan had their rally just before we left Jerusalem. They urged the Sanhedrin to pass even stricter laws not only against marrying into pagan groups, but also against even fraternizing, which can lead to the same thing." Another whispered, "There was even talk about ethnic cleansing, pushing these Samaritans further north where they belong. Weren't they rightfully expelled from the people of God as Nehemiah reports at the end of his memoirs? Oh, it was awful when the son of our high priest married the daughter of Sanballat. Nehemiah fixed 'em as he reported in the last chapter of his book.

*Remember them, O my God, because they have defiled
the priesthood, the covenant of the priests and the
Levites. Thus I cleansed them from everything foreign,
and I established the duties of the priests and Levites,
each in his work....*   — Nehemiah 13:29-30

Oh, Jesus, the time may come when the Serbian Judeans once again cleanse this region of the unclean Samaritans. He sat down all out of breath after making his point so forcefully.

After more training in the new Gospel of Discipleship course, these students of Jesus' teaching would forsake such bigotry and discover a whole new way of seeing people. Later on they would find that Jesus did not hesitate to draw near to "unclean" persons, sick people, disgusting cases of leprosy, a mental case raving with an evil spirit, a rich young ruler, and also a centurion; you name it, Jesus dealt with it, whatever the "it" might be. They would be in the Discipleship Course for several more semesters before they got the point and could see others with a clearer vision.

How Did Jesus See The Samaritan Woman?

Jesus begins the conversation in a remarkably simple and straightforward manner. Nothing about "Please," "You can understand how thirsty I am since I've walked a long way," or "If it's not too much bother, I'd appreciate it if you'd be so kind as to give me a drink since I have neither cup nor bucket." No, it is not even a polite request, but just a bald-faced command: "Give me a drink." And, as was so like him, he almost immediately departs from the mundane topic to a spiritual one: "living water." Now it so happens that this woman had made two bad mistakes. First she got born into a Samaritan family; and second, she fails at one marriage after another. Jesus may well have known this before even addressing her; but he does not focus on this or that stigma, failure, or mistake. He just begins by recognizing her as a person, a person with a bucket that can bring up water from Jacob's well.

The Samaritan woman intuitively recognizes the symbolism of some kind of living water and finally asks a favor in return. She had been to the well often (five times to the marriage well) and had come away still thirsty for a fulfilling life, a refreshing fellowship. Maybe she had not had her thirst quenched at other kinds of wells of life; who knows? The point is that Jesus was not turned off either by her ethnic barrier nor her misfortunes. When she is finally caught in the conversation as Jesus reveals her present situation, Jesus does not bring the law of adultery crashing down upon her head, as he well could have since the Judeans and the Samaritans had had long controversy about how to interpret the Torah (Commandments). He even affirms her by saying, "... and he whom you have is not your husband; this you said truly." Layer after layer of her life unfolds in the conversation to the point where she exclaims that Jesus must be a prophet of some kind.

What kind of impact did Jesus' encounter with the woman have? It was very positive, and very likely quite different from the many negative experiences she had with relatives and neighbors, who would have said, "If I told you once, I've told you a thousand times, if you keep on like this you'll come to no good. You'll end up like a common prostitute the way you're headed." After this fairly brief encounter with Jesus, she rushed back into Sychar and exclaimed, "Come, see a man who told me all that I ever did. Can this be the Christ?" The people must have been amazed that she did not flee from one who knew all this bad stuff about her. Here was the original "tough love," acceptance in spite of blemishes, handicaps, mistakes, failures, and sin. She experienced grace, the grace of God, and knew it. It was good news for her, the good news she wanted to share with others.

The Samaritans also sensed the blessing of Jesus' presence and grace and asked him to stay with them. One wonders how many others got a clearer vision for their lives because of their encounter with this prophet, who could see so clearly all that made up the whole person, the strengths and weaknesses, the shame of group rejection and prejudice as well as the guilt of failures.

How Are We Doing At Seeing The Whole Person?
If a person is below average, handicapped, or has a strike against her/him in the form of a stigma, it is a great relief to be accepted nevertheless. How gratifying it is to such a one to be accepted for

the many other aspects of personality, ability, capacity, and potential even though there are those couple defects or deficiencies. And we all need that since none of us, I believe, is perfect; and even for the perfect one, the very fact of having to be balanced precariously is a problem. Just this past year a cheerleader was so wonderful that she was in danger of being killed out of jealousy.

On page 35 are four exhibits of persons who have something "wrong" with them, a problem to say the least. As you look at these pictures, is the defect the first thing you notice? Does it blot out the rest of the person? Maybe Hester Prynne, in Hawthorne's *Scarlet Letter* (Figure 1), had other qualities like a good singing voice or great skill at weaving. I believe Jesus would have been as inspirational to her as he was to the other Samaritan woman. And, by the way, how would it feel to wear that chain of shame around your neck all day every day?

Figure 2 is myself before I had finished my therapy at the Speech Clinic at the University of Minnesota. Once I had come to accept myself, it became much easier to accept others who were different in some way, maybe missing an arm or leg, confined to a wheelchair, hard of hearing, or blind. Not that we fully understand another, but maybe we are at least less likely to reject the Samaritan woman before us or in the crowd. It is harder for a "perfect" or terribly normal and average person to accept deformity and deficiency. Jesus explained it like this in the case of another Samaritan Woman type. The Pharisees noticed quickly that the woman, anointing Jesus' feet at the dinner table, was a woman of ill repute.

> *If this man were a prophet, he would have known who and what kind of woman this is who is touching him — that she is a sinner ... [Jesus replied] she has shown great love. But the one to whom little is forgiven, [or who has not been accepted] loves little.*
> — Luke 7:39, 47

The little baby in Figure 3 may have very good hearing and perfectly normal arms and legs, but even if we try not to, we stare and are shocked by the startling-looking mouth and distorted nose.

It so happened that this child was very fortunate because surgery did wonders for him. His after surgery photo looks normal with the exception of a slight scar. But I do not show that picture. I want to know if you can love him *before* he is improved. Or do you and I have to wait until he is brought back to normalcy before we say, "Oh, I see this is a child of God, created in God's image." It's a challenge. Every time we can react like Jesus did with the Samaritan woman and others who deviated from normal and ideal, that is another time we are blessing someone and growing in grace a little more ourselves. It is a good feeling when it happens, when grace happens within us by the help of the Holy Spirit.

When I showed Figure 4 to our confirmation class, there was a gasp just like when I showed it to my university Seminar on Stigma. But when I told them she was only twelve years old, there was another audible gasp. I never found out what became of her and if she was helped with this strange medical anomaly, but I know that both classes and I wrestled with our own feelings. Would I have been able to walk up to her in a casual way and say, "Hi, my name is David. What is your name?" As one person with cerebral palsy and a considerably distorted body in a wheelchair said to me, "I wish people would look at me and not just my shell." She would have been happy to have met Jesus because he would have seen the whole person, not just the shell. I am happy to say she belongs to a very supportive church, and she knows Jesus accepts her just as she is. She doesn't have to wait to get better to be loved by God. She's a lot like the Samaritan woman that way. Aren't we all? Amen.

Figure 1. Here comes Hester Prynne with her big Scarlet Letter around her neck.

Figure 2. Stuttering is really not all that attractive. Oh, here he comes again, the one who can't even talk right.

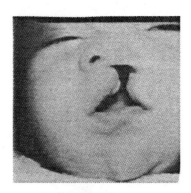

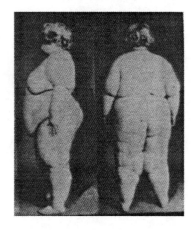

Figure 3. Maybe all you can see is the cleft in his palate. At least it is the first thing you notice. Oh, he was much improved after surgery.

Figure 4. Why does she even come into the swimming pool changing room? You would think she would just stay home. She is twelve years old in this picture.

John 9:1-41
Lent — Week 4

Seeing The Unseeing

Sing along with me:

Amazing grace, how sweet the sound,
That saved a wretch like me!
I once was lost, but now I'm found;
Was blind, but now I see.

This plaintive spiritual song is a favorite among the elderly and nursing home residents at chapel time, those for whom physical eyesight is waning and for whom spiritual sight is increasingly significant. I think many believe it is a Negro spiritual, maybe because of its haunting melody. Actually it was written by John Newton, who was part of the revival of the Church of England in the late eighteenth century. He was a self-educated man, who had gone to sea and at one time had been the captain of a ship in the African slave trade. After his conversion, he became an ordained minister of the Church of England, finally serving as rector of a church in London. It could well be that this personal testimony referred to his time of blindness to the awful exploitation and forced transport of the wretched slaves. He was indeed a spiritual wretch, just as the slaves were physical wretches in the stinking hold of his ship. Through an amazing grace his eyes were opened and he could see clearly God's will for his life, and it was not to haul slaves. Sing it again and imagine you are John Newton. Close your eyes and put yourself in his place.

Amazing grace, how sweet the sound,
That saved a wretch like me!
I once was lost, but now I'm found;
Was blind, but now I see.

It is not only the blind who need to be healed. Most of us could use some therapy to be able to see with a clearer vision what is the holy, the good, the loving, the right path for our pilgrim's progress through life. That's the issue of today's text.

What Did Jesus And The Disciples See?

Jesus saw "a man blind from his birth." No sooner had he seen this than he asked himself, "How can I help this fellow?" It was so typical of Jesus to see a need, to be sensitive to the person before him. Here was an opportunity for service, "... that the works of God might be made manifest in him."

The disciples immediately raised the moralistic question: "Rabbi, who sinned, this man or his parents?" The first task is to fix blame somewhere. Whose fault is it? Sounds familiar. We too are more likely to say, "Who spilled that?" than "Where is a mop so we can wipe it up?" It begins in childhood. "Billy did it, Mom." Before you know it, we are in court; and it's costing us plenty. Recently an outstanding and popular athlete drove his car in front of a large snowplow by entering a state highway where there were no obstructions to vision in either direction. Tragically, the young man was killed. Now a postmortem question of "Whose fault was it?" is being raised. Down the road one can see a lawyer trying to calculate the lifetime earnings of this promising athlete to come up with the damages owed his estate. We are an extremely litigious society and rush to court to find out whose fault it is, "this man or his parents, that he was born blind."

The disciples could certainly have cited many scripture passages dealing with the question of fault and responsibility. Remember in confirmation class hearing this ominous statement as the Ten Commandments were given: "... I the Lord your God am a jealous God, punishing children for the iniquity of parents, to the third and fourth generation of those who reject me." This statement is repeated again in Exodus and in Numbers and Deuteronomy. Not good news to a child born with a congenital birth defect, nor to the child's parents. More times than I like to remember I have heard this dolefully repeated in the hospital with the assumption that this birth defect, this cancer, this curvature of the spine or glaucoma is

38

the punishment for sin, either one's own or that of the parents or grandparents. Oh, it is quite literally true sometimes as when a crack baby suffers from the mother's addiction or some venereal disease results in a serious problem for the offspring. But just because something is sometimes the case does not mean it always is applicable. Jesus said, in this case of the blind man, sin is not an issue, so the disciples might just as well put that out of their minds and focus on something more positive.

A further extension of this principle of retributive justice is the notion that the rich are obviously blessed and the poor always deserve their misfortune. In Malachi we read, "Bring the full tithe ... see if I will not open the windows of heaven for you and pour down for you an overflowing blessing" (Malachi 3:10). Another reason why you may have bad health or many misfortunes is if you come up short in stewardship. Finally, Job was the classic exposition of the thesis that the good prosper and the wicked suffer. A fairly unhelpful counselor, by the name of Eliphaz, comes to Job and says, "Think now, who that was innocent ever perished? Or where were the upright cut off? As I have seen, those who plow iniquity and sow trouble reap the same" (Job 4:7-8). Since Job's children have perished, his oxen have been stolen, his camels carried away, his house destroyed in a windstorm and now his whole body is covered with boils, it is quite obvious he must have sinned grievously. He might as well confess these awful sins deserving of so much punishment. Jesus said quite simply: not so in the case of this blind man.

Go Wash In The Pool Of Siloam

In scripture there is often some symbolic act in connection with a healing. You recall the mighty commander Naaman had a bad case of leprosy. The prophet Elisha did not even meet the great general in person, but sent a messenger with a humble instruction: "Go, wash in the Jordan seven times, and your flesh shall be restored and you shall be clean" (2 Kings 5:10). Boy! Did that make the dignified general mad. He got in his chariot in a huff and drove off cursing, saying, "Are not Abana and Pharpar, the rivers of Damascus, better than all the waters of Israel? Could I not wash in them, and be clean? (5:12). Oh, and another thing, that little prophet didn't even show me the respect to come out and meet me in person. I had big gifts ready to present to him. What an insult!" Then one of his lowly servants timidly offered this observation: "My father, if the prophet had commanded you to do *some great thing*, would you not have done it? How much rather then, when he says to you, 'Wash and be clean'?" (2 Kings 5:13 *RSV*). The moral of the story is this. Commander General Naaman needed to be healed of his *pride* as well as of his leprosy.

What about this Pool of Siloam? Jesus relied upon others who had contributed to this healing at the ancient pool. This pool of water was fed by a remarkable combination of channel and tunnel dug 150 feet deep through solid rock and stretching 1,800 feet from its spring source. We were amazed and impressed to learn that the tunnelers from France and England met exactly on target when completing the passageway under the English Channel, but they had the latest technology. The ancient diggers also began at both ends of this Jerusalem tunnel and also met exactly, as recorded on an inscription found on the tunnel wall in 1880 by some boys in their playful exploring. It goes back to at least 700 B.C. and reads as follows:

> *... This is how the penetration took place. While the diggers were still wielding their axes toward each other, with three cubits (nine feet), they could hear each other shouting, for there was a fissure in the rock running to the south and to the north. So at the moment of penetration, the diggers struck toward each other, axe against axe. Then the waters flowed from the spring to the pool — one thousand two hundred cubits. And one hundred cubits was the height of the rock above the heads of the diggers.*

I could well imagine that as Jesus directed the blind man toward the Pool of Siloam, he also gave thanks for the workers who had made that water available hundreds of years before. Jesus did not hesitate to make use of other people or of the laws of nature to participate in miracles.

I recall that I was grateful to the eye healer, Dr. Hanjoerg Kolder, who replaced my deteriorating lens with a new plastic one. But I also gave thanks to the nurses, inventors, and manufacturers of delicate and incredibly small instruments which the good doctor had available to help him in his work.

Throughout scripture, water has symbolized cleansing, holiness, purification, and regeneration even as we use it in baptism to this day. Thus, the water, the workers, and the words of Jesus blind man. As the story goes, "So he went and washed and came back seeing."

What Are Possible Reactions To A Miracle?

1. It's terrible! It's illegal! That is what the Pharisees knew full well, that you should not work on the sabbath. If you tied a handkerchief to your sash, that was okay because it was part of your clothing, but if you carried it in your hand, it was a burden and that was forbidden labor. The legalistic mind is so often hung up on minute details and technicalities. Oh, healing is fine and good in its place, but absolutely do not do it on the sabbath. Jesus brushed all that aside with his famous remark that the sabbath was made for persons and not that persons were made for the sabbath. The same could be said about most policy and procedure manuals, governmental regulations, and fine print of endless documents. We're not only disappointed that a so-called religious leader would heal on the sabbath; we're outraged and disgusted. It's really too bad this blind man can see.

2. "The Jews did not believe that he had been blind and had received his sight...." We have a saying, "It's too good to be true." What is there about us that so often doubts that good things could or would happen? Even in our daily evening news, there are nine bad things announced for every one good thing that is reported. This house burned down. Two children were eaten by a wild dog. Clerk injured in Quik Trip as thief escapes with unknown amount of money. Two more clergy charged with sex abuse of women parishioners. Four senators and three representatives found guilty of graft, bribery, and assorted malfeasance of office are sentenced to a prison with only one golf course and six tennis courts. Volcano

41

buries 500 natives. Serbs rape and murder another 350 women. Car bomb in Belfast kills six in shopping center. Oh, yes, by the way, a school teacher in Twin Oaks received an award as best debate coach in the state. That ends our evening news. Tune in again tomorrow morning for more helpful information. Let's investigate this so-called healing; maybe we'll get lucky and find out it did not happen.

3. The parents felt themselves in the middle when they were asked to take a stand. They more or less said, "Leave us out of it." John reports they said, "Ask him; he is of age, he will speak for himself." They feared they would be put out of the synagogue if they showed an inclination to believe in the Christ. It was beyond the memory of many here that Senator Joe McCarthy of Wisconsin made threats like that. And today we have "political correctness." It happened in Jesus' day; it happens today and it always happens. One might have to pay a price for taking a stand.

4. What of the man who was healed? No doubt he had been reduced to sitting at the gate of some street corner with a cup, begging for his meager support. He was not only healed but greatly strengthened. He spoke right up to his betters, the more educated leaders of the religious community, and said, "Why, this is a marvel! You do not know where he comes from, and yet he opened my eyes" (John 9:30). He was cast out of the synagogue, and I doubt if he cared one whit. Consider the source. It may even be a positive testimony if genuine knuckleheads reject you. His next encounter with Jesus brought out this testimony of faith: "Lord, I believe."

A Strange Paradox:
The Blind See And Those Who See Become Blind

Once again Jesus turns things around and reverses our usual way of looking at things. He summed up the meaning of this whole incident: "For judgment I came into this world, that those who do not see may see, and that those who see may become blind" (John 9:39). When Jesus was describing the moral bankruptcy of the hypocritical Pharisees, he used the metaphor of blindness: "... they are blind guides of the blind. And if one blind person guides another, both will fall into the pit." To some Pharisees who stayed on to question him after he made the remark above, he made this statement: "If you were blind [like a sociopath who can't distinguish right from wrong], you would have no guilt; but now that you say, 'We see [understand the spiritual issue],' your guilt remains" (John 9:41 *RSV*). One really needs to wrestle with Jesus' words here as they might pertain to one's own life. I suppose that those who can see physically feel really glad about that, satisfied, one might say. Remember John Newton, the slave trafficker, before his conversion had to have very good physical vision in order to be a captain of a ship, to see the North Star, and read the navigational maps of his day. But one day he realized that good eyesight was leading him on a dangerous course. He might gain riches but lose his soul. Although he could see with his eyeballs, his soul was blind. Once he discovered his spiritual handicap, he had a clearer vision for his life as a whole. He could truly see in the more important sense. Let us close by reflecting again upon the meaning of John Newton's verse.

> *Amazing grace, how sweet the sound,*
> *That saved a wretch like me!*
> *I once was lost, but not I'm found;*
> *Was blind, but now I see. Amen.*

Seeing Light In Darkness

As death drew near for a seventy-year-old man, a cousin was heard to say to his wife, "Don't worry, Agatha, it seems dark now, but in time you'll see the light at the end of this tunnel." Some use another cliche, "It's always darkest before the dawn." These are not helpful statements. And Agatha, about to become a widow, simply sighs and says to herself, "No one understands."

It may have seemed to the sisters, Martha and Mary, that Jesus did not understand the seriousness of Lazarus' illness. Here their brother is dying and Jesus delays two whole days in coming to their aid.

Should The Dying Always Be Healed?
Should The Dead Always Be Brought Back To Life?

Obviously not. Of the hundreds of thousands of Jews who died, how many were brought back? Scarce few. Of the thousands who were sick unto death, how many were rescued at the last minute by miraculous healing? Scarce few. None of the disciples (especially Judas). Some of them died of martyrdom and maybe some of just plain old age. The vast majority of Jews lived and died according to the laws of nature, being healthy or catching a disease; dying after a long life or being kicked in the head in the teens by a camel.

It is only in recent modern times that we have hoped or been able to control and postpone death with such success. Even today such "heroic measures" are called "extraordinary means": the pumps, suctions, drips, respirators, heart/lung machines, dialysis, defibrillators, machinery and powerful technology, wonder drugs, CAT scans and magnetic imaging diagnostic gadgets — the list grows longer each month as inventors and researchers strive mightily to stave off death.

Finally, the State of Oregon has said that this mad race with death must stop. It has gotten totally out of hand and out of proportion. In order to prevent some rare cases from dying, we must deprive a hundred thousand or more of even basic health care. The vast majority of our health care costs are spent in the last months of life (surely not the most rewarding) as we lie in an intensive care hospital bed surrounded by an array of life support systems keeping our unconscious body metabolizing with artificial breathing devices and tube feedings maintaining a minimum physical existence. Not only is this unrewarding; it is often not even therapeutic. Yes, we are being forced to confront the darkness of death and accept it as a reality.

In the recent past decades we have rediscovered the value and necessity of going through the darkness of grieving and mourning. Rather than denying the fact of death by glossing it over with repression and relabeling, we are encouraged to experience and express the darkness and sorrow that death of a beloved person brings to us. We no longer use phrases such as "He's departed" (like United flight #206 has departed for Chicago). We simply say, "Lars died Wednesday and we buried him Friday at West Branch Cemetery." In church, at the grave site, and back at the church fellowship, tears of loss are acceptable. And we do not offer cheap cliches to soften the reality.

What if we could not die? What if death did not exist? Would that be a good thing? How long until China's population would be six billion or New York City would have a population of 89 million? What if flies and mosquitoes never died? They would be ankle deep in the yard and driveway. Nature would have to be totally reorganized on some other principle. The life cycle implies a beginning and an end. The Letter to the Hebrews implies as much in this cryptic phrase: "... it is appointed to mortals to die...." Being mortal means that death will be in the picture sooner or later for all of us.

Just as death is always inevitable, there is also an undeniable darkness about it; an ominous bleakness about it makes us cringe and draw back. It is only natural that Martha and Mary wished it had been otherwise. "Martha said to Jesus, 'Lord, if you had been here, my brother would not have died.' " Not only were Martha and Mary weeping, the neighbors and relatives were likewise in sorrow. And John reports simply, "Jesus wept." It was a dark time for everyone.

Why Did Jesus Raise Lazarus?

Nowhere does it say that Jesus did this for Lazarus' benefit. There is no report that Lazarus said, "Thank you, Lord." Nor that he was pleased to be brought back only to have to die another time. There is also nothing in the story to indicate that Jesus brought Lazarus back for the benefit of Martha and Mary. Maybe Lazarus was the only source of financial support of his sisters. Women, after all, were not very employable in Bible times. No, this economic benefit is not stated in the story.

What of the fellowship and companionship of their brother? Jesus did not even suggest, "Yes, I realize you would miss Lazarus in your family circle, at mealtime and at family reunions; therefore, I will restore him to you for your social comfort." No. He did not give this reason even though Jesus would also miss him. Jesus referred to the dead man as "our friend Lazarus." And he himself wept at the loss. Not only would Jesus have blessed the sisters but himself with the restoration of Lazarus to their midst. But no, this socio-emotional and personal benefit is not mentioned as a reason for raising Lazarus.

Jesus states quite clearly four times in this short story the purpose and meaning of this miraculous raising of Lazarus:

... it is for the glory of God (v. 4).

... so that you may believe (v. 5).

Did I not tell you that if you believe you would see the glory of God? (v. 40).

... on account of the people standing by (v. 42).

Jesus, ever the teacher, adds a moral or lesson to healings and other works of wonder. To one patient he said, after the healing, that she should go and sin no more. The goal that she needed to attain was to learn the need to change her life. If she learned that lesson, the healing was well worth it. To this very day physicians throw up their hands when patients come back again and again because of their illness-producing behavior. We call it recidivism.

47

Jesus used signs and wonders to open people's eyes and to foster their faith — an early example of audiovisual aids in teaching. But Jesus looked upon these as means to an end and not ends in themselves. For example, he once seemed a bit put out that people just wanted to be entertained without getting the lesson straight. In the sixteenth chapter of Matthew, we have this encounter with the Pharisees and Sadducees: "... and to test him they asked him to show them a sign from heaven." Jesus rebuked them, "An evil and adulterous generation asks for a sign...." And to the official at Capernaum, whose son was ill, Jesus said, "Unless you see signs and wonders you will not believe."

Seeing Light In Darkness

First off, let us agree that the solution is not to deny darkness, whether it be fatal illness, debilitating illness, unemployment, loss of loved one through death, or loss of status through unemployment.

Once a deteriorating man sat across from me in a most despairing state of mind. He shared that he had just now come from a park with a swiftly flowing river where he had sat for four hours trying to decide whether to drown himself. He was in that much darkness. He finally was able to see the light through Alcoholics Anonymous. He found a Power greater than himself and became a new person. It was as though Jesus had said to him, "Come out; come out of your cave of isolation and despair." And Jesus said to the fellow alcoholics in his squad meeting, "Unbind him, and let him go." Let him go back into life. He's been dead long enough.

Jesus was more concerned about spiritual darkness than physical darkness. You remember last Sunday how he spoke about the paradox of the seeing and the blind: "... For judgment I came into this world, that those who do not see may see, and that those who see may become blind." One may see very well in the marketplace of shrewd practices or in the political arena of one's lost integrity, and even appear to prosper according to the values of this world. But what if in the process one descended into spiritual darkness? In the tenth chapter of Matthew Jesus speaks of this plainly.

What I tell you in the dark, utter in the light; and what
you hear whispered, proclaim upon the housetops. And
do not fear those who kill the body but cannot kill the
soul; rather fear him who can destroy both soul and
body in hell. — Matthew 10:27-28 *RSV*

Can we take this stance? Can we have less fear of death whether
we are killed by cancer, old age, car accident, war, or an intruder
into our home than we have fear of losing our integrity, our identity, and our personhood?

Jesus did not hesitate to head directly into what anyone, especially his disciples, would know were dark days ahead. His disciples doubted if he should even go back to where Martha and
Mary were grieving and where Lazarus lay, in Bethany on the very
outskirts of Jerusalem, from where Jesus had just recently escaped
within an inch of his life. "Rabbi, the Jews were but now seeking
to stone you, and are you going there again?" His reply:

Are there not twelve hours in the day? If anyone walks
in the day, he does not stumble, because he sees the
light of this world. But if anyone walks in the night, he
stumbles, because the light is not in him.
— John 11:9-10 *RSV*

Fascinating! Maybe the light is not at the end of the tunnel; rather
it is "in" oneself. The Quakers refer to the "Inner Light." Faith is
inside a person, not out there somewhere. We read about the Spirit
dwelling in us, guiding us and sanctifying us.

Jesus pressed on to Jerusalem because he had a resurrection
faith that would sustain him even though his body would be put to
death. That light guided and empowered him even unto his own
darkness of Good Friday.

We have spoken of "inner light" as the inward experience of
faith and confidence. But there is another symbolism. In John's
Gospel there is a testimony as to the nature of the Christ who came
into the world at Christmas. It is not the warm Sunday school program story of the shepherds and wise men and the baby Jesus lying

49

in the manger. It is more philosophical and deals with the coming into the world of the True Wisdom and the True Light. It goes like this:

> *In the beginning was the Word, and the Word was with God, and the Word was God ... What has come into being in him was life, and the life was the light of all people. The light shines in the darkness, and the world did not overcome it ... The true light, which enlightens everyone, was coming into the world.*
>
> — John 1:1, 3-5, 9

Thus the Christ is a beacon guiding us through an often dark journey even through death. Jesus said to Martha, "I am the resurrection, and the life: he that believeth in me, though he were dead, yet shall he live." That would be the lot of Lazarus in the long run, for Martha, for Jesus himself, and for us.

For some cultures light is very significant, especially in northern countries where it is a scarce item during many months. I think of a beloved Danish hymn, which captures the lifesaving function of light. On this island country surrounded by the rough seas, there are lighthouses to guide the fishermen and crews of merchant freighters, who are hoping to make it safe to the harbor at last. What a welcome sight is the blinking light indicating the safe entrance to the harbor and home.

Aaberg has a verse in a Danish hymnal that I don't find anywhere else:

> **"Vor Fader har Lys i sit Vindue."**
> *Our Father has light in His window,*
> *It shines through the darkening night*
> *And carries a friendly greeting*
> *To all from the Lord of light*
>
> *Our Father has light in His window,*
> *It brightens the darkest road,*
> *It comforts in need and sorrow*
> *And points us the way to God.*

Our Father has light in his window,
It beckons thro' storm and gloam
And, beaming with loving kindness,
It bids us: Come home, come home!

Whether a young cabin boy who had run away from home to go to sea, or a seasoned captain back from another long sea journey, or a rugged old salt who was almost accustomed to such long absences from home and family — all on board were glad to see the harbor light. That is truly seeing light in the darkness. When we are tempted to focus only on the darkness, may we pray for light enough for our journey until we also come safe to the harbor at last. Amen.